# IT'S NEVER

# TO FIND A NEW WAY OF

# LIFE

**David S Smith**

## ACKNOWLEDGEMENTS

I wish to express my deep gratitude to my friend, Pastor Peter Ayrton, for his encouragement and support in the writing of this book and his editorial contributions.

Also, I give my warm thanks to Rosemarie Ayrton for all her hard work typing and preparing the manuscripts, and for her lovely illustration. My heartfelt thanks also go to my friends Julie Fox, Stella Burgoyne, John Tuck and my wife Wendy who contributed their own illustrations to this book.

I am very grateful to Paul Bate and John Buckeridge for being my additional editors and for their very helpful comments and suggestions.

Finally, I would like to express my thanks and appreciation to everyone at Amazon Publishing for the publication of my book.

# INDEX

First Introduction

Second Introduction

Chapter 1 - The big questions of life

Chapter 2 - My background

Chapter 3 - The start of my journey

Chapter 4 - A spiritual experience

Chapter 5 - The evidence for Jesus

Chapter 6 - Then a funny thing happened on the way to happiness

Chapter 7 - New life with the Holy Spirit

Chapter 8 - Understanding the Fruits of the Spirit

Chapter 9 - The existence of God

Chapter 10 - Having a personal relationship with God

Chapter 11 - What about church ?

Chapter 12 - Hope for the future

Chapter 13 - Can I rekindle my faith ?

Chapter 14 - In Conclusion : Your future starts now !


Appendix 1 - The song

Appendix 2 - The Parables of Jesus

## FIRST INTRODUCTION

As I sit down at home and start to write this book, the whole of mankind, not just in the UK but throughout the whole world, is in the middle of a terrible pandemic called Covid-19 virus. This is a new virus to attack humans and led to the end of normal life as we knew it.

I do not propose to go into too much detail about Covid-19 virus, as other books and sources of information on this subject are available.

Suffice to say, it is believed the virus started in the street market at Wuhan, China at the end of 2019 and quickly spread to most other countries, Europe and the UK by the early part of 2020. Many thousands of people have died and millions have contracted the virus and suffered health problems.

This led the British Government and devolved authorities of Scotland, Wales and Northern Ireland to bring in strict measures and regulations, in an attempt to control the spread of the virus, to save lives and avoid the NHS hospitals from being overwhelmed.

The Government's main action, in March 2020, was to enforce a "lockdown", ordering the closure of shops, pubs, cinemas, schools, theatres, churches, village halls, all sports activities and other places where people gather together. People were also told to work from home where possible.

This action appeared to work initially, when infection rates started to fall, but after "lockdown" ended in August/September 2020 a "second wave" of infections reared its ugly head, causing the Government to bring back the severe restrictions in October 2020, this time on a regional level.

The rate of new infections did not come down, however and people were only allowed to meet one other household at Christmas, for one day only. Then a new mutation of Covid-19 started sweeping the country, spreading more quickly and pushing new infection rates to over 50,000 per day!

This led the Government to introduce a new total lockdown from the 6th January 2021.

There is light at the end of the tunnel, as scientists have developed a vaccine and we have embarked on a UK/worldwide vaccination programme.

So the result of these "lockdown" regulations is that most people were (and perhaps still are) mainly confined to their own homes and seeking new ways to spend their time.

The use of computers and the internet has increased greatly during this time. People are turning to online retail and food shopping, online education for children when schools are closed, online community support and online church services. Many people have also started working from home and holding meetings online through programmes like Zoom. Families have also seen and talked together on their computers.

Does this sound familiar to you ?

If so, this book is for you. This could now be the best time in your life to reflect upon how you have lived prior to the Covid-19 pandemic. How your life was changed and what you would like your future to look like.

# SECOND INTRODUCTION

# THE LIGHTER SIDE OF GROWING OLDER

The rapid spread of the Covid-19 virus, a killer virus and the effects of Government restrictions and lockdowns, have left many people with mental health issues, depression, anxiety and sadness.

We all desperately need cheering up ! We need to hug, laugh and have fun with family and friends again.

Getting older - say over the age of 50 - doesn't have to be a worry, or sad. We still have a lot to live for, to look forward to and have fun in your "new life".

So I have included here some "jokes for seniors" to lift up your spirits.

1. You know you're getting old when the candles cost more than the cake.

2. What's the worst part about retiring? You never get a day off work!

3. I'm at an age when my back goes out more than I do.

4. Why don't old people eat health food? They need all the preservatives they can get!

5. A senior citizen was driving on the motorway when his wife rings. She says, "Just heard on the news there is a car going the wrong way on the motorway, please be careful". The man replies, "Heck, it's not just one car, it's hundreds of them".

6. I was at a cash machine the other day when an old lady came up to me and asked me to help her check her balance - so I pushed her over!

7. My memory is not as good as it used to be. And also, my memory is not as good as it used to be.

8. Older people are like computers - we start out with lots of memory and drive, then we become outdated and crash (sleep) at odd moments and eventually have our parts replaced!

# CHAPTER 1

# THE BIG QUESTIONS OF LIFE

Let us start by asking yourself the BIG questions of life itself:

Can I really find a new and better way of life? A better "new normal".

What is my purpose in life anyway - what am I doing here?

Who am I - the real me?

What happens to my soul when I die?

Do I want a more loving, caring, kinder community and world in which to live?

I cannot, of course, answer these questions for you as they are personal to each one of us to discover for ourselves. The purpose of this book is to encourage you to start your own journey of discovery.

Because I found myself in this exact same position in 2006/7 asking questions about my life. I will start by sharing with you my own personal story, why I wanted to discover the meaning of life and find answers to these other big questions. I will explain how I set about doing that, leading to the amazing spiritual experience I had in May 2007 and how that has changed and improved my life considerably.

My sole aim in writing this book is so that you too will find and enjoy the better way of life, the Christian way, which I found for myself at the ripe old age of 63. As I said before, it is never too late!

In other words, this book is not only my personal testimony, but an easy and simple to read "guide book" to finding a real purpose in life, a faith, with joy, happiness and contentment.

But before I get into the "nitty gritty" of what happened in May 2007, and my experiences since, let me give you some background of my life up to the age of 63.

# CHAPTER 2

## MY BACKGROUND

I was born in Hackney Hospital, East London, on the 30th January, 1944 amidst the German bombing raids on London (and many other towns) in the second world war.

My father, Stanley, was serving in the British Army, somewhere in France, so shortly after my birth my mother Jessie took me to stay with her sister in Blackburn, Lancashire, where we stayed until the war ended in 1945.

We then moved back to live with my dad's mother in Hackney until 1947 when my parents were given a "prefab" bungalow in Loughton, Essex, by London County Council. After two more years we then moved to a council house in Old Harlow, Essex in 1949. In the September of 1949 I started my Primary School education at Fawbert Barnards School in Old Harlow.

During the summer of 1955, when I was then aged 11, my parents moved back to live in East London and took over the tenancy of a Taylor Walker Public House in Bethnal Green. We lived in the residential rooms above the pub. I started to attend Mansford Secondary School, where I stayed until leaving at the age of 16 years.

With no academic or university education behind me, I was not sure what type of jobs or work to consider, but my father had a friend who worked as a solicitor's clerk and this had a certain appeal to me. In April 1959 I started my first career in the legal profession, as a junior clerk at a firm of solicitors in London, W1. Several months later, I went on to join another firm in Fleet Street, London. I continued working in the legal profession for 20 years, passing many exams and qualifying as a Legal Executive by Diploma.

My parents were never "church goers" or religious in any way, shape or form, so I was brought up as an atheist. Some people, of course, are born into an existing Christian family (or other faiths) but I believe that since the 1960's onwards, the majority of us have not, and therefore have grown up without learning all about the Christian faith, or the real presence of God in our lives.

In the Spring of 1962, when I was 18, I met a girl who lived in North London and after "going out" for a short while she told me she was pregnant! This put me in a state of shock and confusion, and in those days, unlike the present time, there was great stigma and shame over a single, unmarried girl becoming pregnant. Consequently, under great pressure from both sets of parents, we were married in October 1962. I have two lovely children from this marriage, but eventually this broke down and we were divorced in 1971.

After a chance meeting with a couple of business men at the end of 1979, who were both managers working for a large financial services company in London, and after several further meetings with them, I decided to make a career change and work in the world of Financial Services from early 1980.

Our work ethos was "work hard, play hard" so my life became very busy.

My work in Financial Services included being based in London and later in the Home Counties.

However, I did suffer an early set-back when, in September 1980, whilst playing golf I collapsed on the course and was taken by ambulance to hospital with a ruptured spleen. My spleen was removed and I was off work for 3 months.

In October 1986 I married a dance teacher and my third lovely child was born in December 1989.

I continued to work hard until the end of 2004, when I experienced a lack of drive and motivation, coupled with a loss of interest in my work, and sometimes in life itself; the common symptoms of depression. This led me to retire from work in January 2005 at the age of 61.

# CHAPTER 3

## THE START OF MY JOURNEY

Like many people in the capitalist western world, my focus was on the pursuit of personal success, material possessions and money, with very little time to reflect and contemplate a better way of life.

The problem with this self-centred focus, I found that it does not give you complete satisfaction, or contentment with your life. Enough is never enough. We always want more and live in fear of losing what we have. There is a well-known saying, "The grass is greener on the other side of the road".

But, having now retired from work at the "young" age of 61, what to do next?

I believe that what happened next was the actual source, the start of my Christian life journey. I think of it as like a river, which from its small source flows and grows over many miles into a large, strong river, full of life.

One of my friends, Peter, is an undertaker and in June 2005 he approached me with regard to a vacancy coming up, for Office

Manager/Funeral Arranger at one of his offices. Whilst I now felt ready to do something completely different, I was not sure about working with dead bodies!

At Peter's suggestion, I started working alongside him, at his own office, for a couple of weeks. I quickly discovered that helping people and families in a caring, compassionate way, during their time of grieving, was highly satisfying. Needless to say, I agreed to take the job.

I was based at Peter's "office" in Gerrards Cross, Buckinghamshire, where we had a main meeting/interview room, with a door leading into a smaller side room used for viewing of the deceased person, in the coffin, by family and friends. From the front door a passage led into a back room admin office, where all the funeral arranging work was done, which in turn led into the "mortuary" room containing eight refrigerated units.

So, back to the start of my Christian journey. This happened when, one day in early 2007, a man walked into my office "off the street" and asked if it was possible to arrange his own funeral before his death. He explained to me that he was a widower and that he had a terminal illness, with only a few more months to live. He said he did not wish to burden his two daughters with making all the funeral arrangements.

After confirming to him that this was indeed possible, I took him into the main meeting room and started to record the details of the church funeral he wanted. We then had two or three further meetings to clarify and confirm final details.

I next saw this man in March/April 2007 when he was brought into me, in a body bag, having passed away in hospital. As I was preparing him in his coffin, I could not help thinking about our meetings and conversations just a few weeks earlier.

I began to wonder and think about what is missing when we die? Is it just our heartbeat, or do we have a soul? If we have a soul which leaves our body when we die, where does it go? In other words, is there an after-life in heaven?

Then, so many questions flashed through my mind. The BIG questions that I mentioned earlier in this book. For several days I thought and pondered upon these questions, but did not know who, or where to go to, to get my answers.

Then amazingly at the next church funeral I conducted I picked up a leaflet inside the church saying, "Discover the Meaning of Life, Attend an Alpha Course".

My curiosity started working overtime and I thought - yes, I do want to discover the meaning of life. From a young child I have always had an inquisitive mind (but then again, don't we all?) and often thought about the stars in the sky, the universe and whether there was life on any other planets. More about this later.

I had not heard of Alpha before so I started asking around and I then discovered that Little Kingshill Baptist Church, in Bucks, was starting a new Alpha Course in May 2007, led by their Minister, Colin Pye, and Assistant Minister, Heather McIntyre. Whilst at that time I thought I was not interested in attending church, they explained the meetings would be held in the separate hall, on one evening each week, over 10 weeks and it started with a free hot meal. My good friend Peter, the undertaker, lived in Little Kingshill and I had previously met Colin Pye on a few occasions at Peter's "infamous" BBQ parties. I therefore felt comfortable I could go, at least to the first meeting, and ask some of the many questions in my mind about the spiritual world, life after death and improving my life on earth. There was also, of course, the free meal to enjoy!

So, decision made, I went along to the first introductory session at the Church Hall on 25th April, 2007. There were about 20 other people there and we were put on tables of four, plus one or two others on each table from the church community, who had prepared and served the food. At the back end of the hall was a large screen, on which we watched a DVD film, which was then followed by a discussion and question time.

Much to my surprise, I found the meeting to be very friendly, informal and informative, so I attended the next meeting/session on 9th May, 2007. This was the first proper Session 1 of the course and we were all given an Alpha Course booklet. After watching another DVD film and asking a few questions, my curiosity about my purpose in life and the Christian faith got stronger.

It was when I attended Session 2 on the 16th May, 2007 that I had what can only be described as a spiritual experience or encounter, which completely transformed my life after this date.

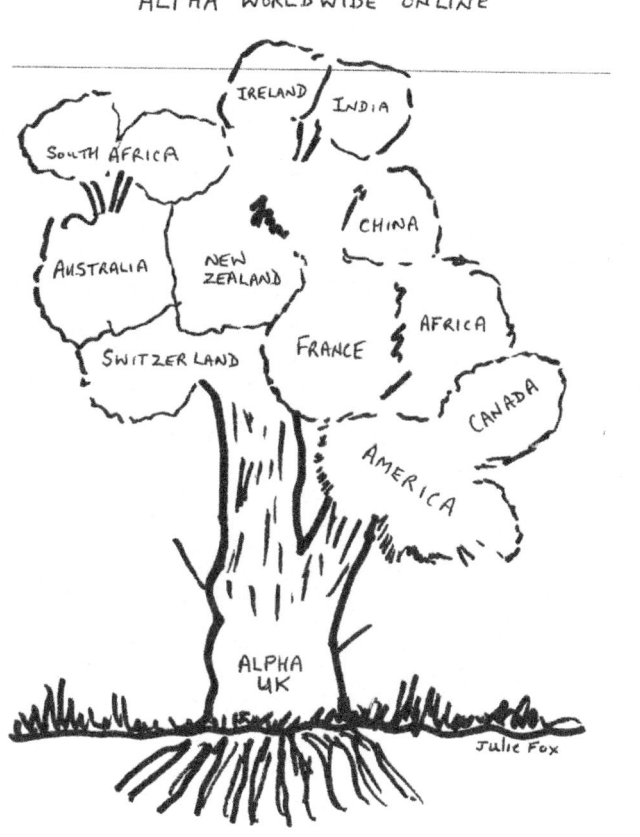

## CHAPTER 4

## A SPIRITUAL EXPERIENCE

We all experience many situations, events and circumstances in our lifetimes, most of which we can explain away, but a spiritual experience is something very different, which is not caused or instigated by "man" but comes from the spiritual world, namely God.

This type of experience is harder to explain, but I will do my best, in an honest and truthful way.

On that evening of 16th May, 2007, as I walked into the Church Hall, the first thing I saw was Heather McIntyre standing at the far end of the hall, and I saw a bright aura of light over and around her head and she was smiling. I was totally mesmerized at this sight and instead of going to my table, I walked over to speak with her. As I stood there, I immediately felt a "glow" pass through my body. I now believe it was at that moment I received the gift of the Holy Spirit from God, but more about that in a later chapter.

I then took my place at the table and, after enjoying the customary hot meal, watched the third DVD film. At the previous week - Session 1 - we had discussed the question "Who is Jesus?" and at this Session 2 the film, and group discussions, focused on the question, "Why Did Jesus Die?".

When I woke up the next morning I still felt the inner glow, but I also felt somehow different. As I mentioned before, some things are hard to explain, all I can say is I felt an immense peace within myself and a desire to find out more about Jesus. But what made me feel so different? Another question in my mind to answer! As I say, more about that in a later chapter.

# CHAPTER 5

# THE EVIDENCE FOR JESUS

Because of my legal background and experience of court work, I wanted to find the proof, the evidence, not only of Jesus' existence, but also the miracles He performed, His crucifixion and resurrection. Was Jesus really the Son of God?

I do not wish to bore you with a long history lesson, but what I discovered was that the Roman Empire ruled over much of Europe and the Middle East 2020 years ago, including the region where Jesus Christ lived. The Romans were excellent scribes and some of their historical documents still exist today. For example, Cornelius Tacitus was a Roman historian who wrote and published Annals, in which he explicitly states that Nero persecuted the Christians, and also that Jesus Christ was put to death by Pontius Pilate.

I also found that a Jewish historian named Josephus, who lived circa 37-100 AD, published "Jewish Antiquities", a history of the Jews in twenty books. In this historical record, Jesus of Nazareth, along with His brother James and John the Baptist are all mentioned.

This is clear proof that Jesus Christ really existed.

But what about the so-called miracles that Jesus performed, which could only be "supernatural acts". Where is the evidence for those?

During my research and initial transition from Atheist to the Christian faith, I discovered that Jesus performed many "miracles" (beyond human power) that were written down and recorded. Most people will have heard of and know some of these, including Jesus walking on water, Jesus turning 5 loaves and 2 fish into food for 5000 people, Jesus turning water into wine and Jesus healing many people with blindness, disabilities and illness/injury.

These "wonderful works" of Jesus are not only recorded in the "Jewish Antiquities" books, but also in many scrolls and parchments discovered by archaeologists between 1838 to 1961. And we have all heard of "The Dead Sea Scrolls" haven't we? All these miracles could not possibly have happened without the "hand of God".

In addition to these recent archaeological discoveries, there were much older records (apart from those written by Roman historians) from eye witnesses of the miracles, describing these events.

For example, there was a Jewish fisherman named John, who lived in the town of Capernaum (in Northern Israel) which is where Jesus spent most of his last 3 years. John not only wrote a biography of Jesus, he also wrote three letters to the followers of Jesus.

Then there was Matthew, a Jewish tax collector, also from Capernaum. After meeting and following Jesus, he also wrote about His life and miracles.

Another fisherman named Peter became a follower of Jesus and was a witness to His resurrection from death on a Roman cross and burial. Many other people also saw Jesus, days after His death!

And my final example is a man called Paul (formerly named Saul). After gaining a reputation of a chief persecutor of the followers of Jesus, he encountered a spiritual experience whilst travelling to Damascus. As a result, Paul became one of the most outspoken supporters of Jesus and wrote many letters and documents.

At this time, over 2000 years ago, most ordinary people could not read or write and heard about Jesus through "word of mouth". Then in 367 AD a big meeting was held, when all these historical records, scrolls and parchments were gathered together and considered. This meeting was called The Council of Nicaea. They later consolidated these writings into 66 books, which we know as the Christian Bible.

My search for the evidence, the truth of what I had heard, led me to the indisputable conclusion that "history does not lie" and the Bible is an accurate and thrilling account of God's plan for the human race, from beginning of creation to the end of the world and everything written about Jesus is true and Holy.

If you believe in the truth of other ancient historical records, such as of Vikings invasion of Europe, William the Conqueror 1066, Kings and Queens of England, Explorers of old and many, many other individual lives featured in world events, how can anyone not believe in Jesus or the Bible?

Later in this book, in Chapter 9, I explain how God, in his creation of human beings, gave us freedom of choice. We are free to follow God's commands, or not.

The same goes for your belief in Jesus Christ. Jesus said, "Whoever is not with me is against me" (Matthew 12 : 30). In other words, we cannot "sit on the fence".

If you accept Jesus Christ your past sins (mistakes) are forgiven and, by God's grace, you are given everlasting life. This is your "Golden Ticket" to heaven.

But more than that, your life is made full, instead of empty or lacking and very meaningful.

# CHAPTER 6

# THEN A FUNNY THING HAPPENED (ON THE WAY TO HAPPINESS)

I continued attending the subsequent sessions of the Alpha Course and at Session 4 we discussed why, and how, we should pray. I don't mind admitting that at that time praying was something very new to me.

My main pastime, when not working, was playing golf at my local golf club. My first game after Session 4 was a knockout club competition match. My opponent was a good player and I prayed that I would play well - and won the game! Well, the prayer worked, I won, and went into the next round. Then in the next round, the same thing happened, and I thought WOW - Thank you God! Just before playing in the third round, I felt a "whisper" in my ear. Someone (the Holy Spirit) was saying, "David, are you being a bit selfish and not considering others in your prayers?". Yes, I thought, can't argue with that, so before starting to play against an opponent with a higher handicap (which means I was a better player) I simply prayed that he, my opponent, would play well. As it turned out he played very well, hitting all his shots and his putting falling into the holes from all directions! He won the match. As we walked from the last green to the club house, he turned to me and said, "I don't know what happened there, but that is the best I have every played in all my life". I thought to myself - ah, I know what happened, God listened and answered my prayers.

Another funny thing happened, towards the end of the Alpha Course, in about July 2007. As I woke up one morning, I suddenly had the words of a song come into my mind. The reason I thought this was very strange is that I am not, and never had been, very musical. Yes, like most people, I sometimes listen to music, pop songs and programmes on the radio, or CD player at home, but I have never been able to play the piano or other musical instrument.

I then got up and wrote down on paper the words of this song. I had the tunes of two pop songs buzzing through my head as I was writing the words, which were "In the Army Now" by Status Quo and "I Want to Break Free" by Queen.

I have included the lyrics of the song as Appendix 1 at the back of this book, but it is lacking an original tune or music, so if any readers are also musical and can compose the tune, I would love to hear from you.

## CHAPTER 7

## NEW LIFE WITH THE HOLY SPIRIT

Having now completed the Alpha Course, and feeling my attitude to life, and God, had changed, what now? How do I want to live the rest of my life?

I had made some new friends on the Alpha Course and decided to attend Little Kingshill Baptist Church, to learn more. I saw "church" as being about people and new friends sharing a common interest, and not about the building or "religion".

What surprised me the most about starting to attend church was how friendly, and fun, it was. Instead of singing old traditional hymns (I have nothing against these hymns as many are very well known and beautiful in themselves) they had a group of musicians and we would normally sing "praise songs". The Minister, Colin Pye, played lead guitar and there was also an electric keyboard, bass guitar, wind instruments and drums.

Singing these songs gave me a great sense of joy and a love for singing.

Of course there was also the serious and important side of prayers and Colin's sermons, but they were always applicable to living our lives today. The service was always followed by coffee/tea and biscuits and chat with friends.

I also joined a weekly post-Alpha home group, run by Heather McIntyre, which gave us more opportunities for friendly discussion and to explore the teachings of Jesus, leading to the new life worth living.

A wonderful life-changing "bonus" for me was also meeting a lovely new friend , Wendy, who later became my wife. We were married at Little Kingshill Baptist Church in September 2011.

I can speak from my own spiritual experience, described earlier, that when someone becomes a Christian, God's Holy Spirit comes to dwell in their heart and mind. This is explained in the Bible, in Romans 8 : 9.

In Chapter 4 of this book I asked the question, "What made me feel so different?". This important question is also dealt with on the Alpha Course and the answer is that the Holy Spirit transforms us from within.

I believe we are all born with, and develop over our lives, basic feelings, characters and something called our "disposition". We start with a selfish, impatient, sinful nature and our general behaviour, attitude to others, how we treat family and friends, how we drive, are all affected by our disposition.

When the Holy Spirit entered into my life my old feelings were replaced with a new concern for others and a feeling of happiness, peace, patience, goodness and self control.

Now I ask you, who would not want to experience that for themselves?

This new life with the Holy Spirit, living by the Spirit's power, is fully set out in the Bible - Galatians 5 : 16-26. Verse 22 tells us that when the Holy Spirit lives within us, and guides our lives, we produce "Fruits of the Spirit" which are :- Love, Joy, Peace, Patience, Kindness, Goodness, Faithfulness, Gentleness and Self-Control.

If you ever wondered where our thoughts, our feelings, our emotions - all these good, positive, invisible states of the heart and mind come from, now you know.

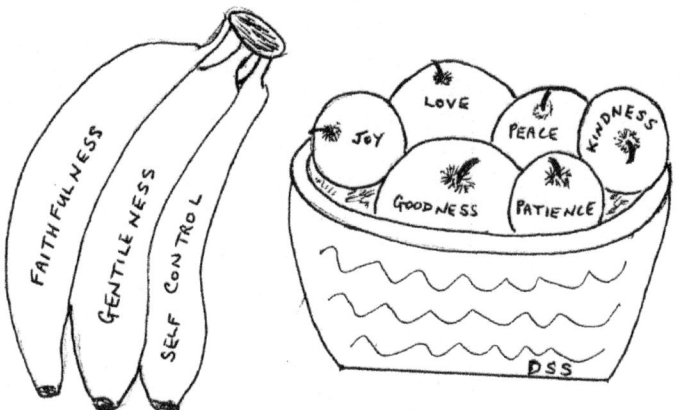

## CHAPTER 8

## UNDERSTANDING THE FRUITS OF THE SPIRIT

There are many places in the Bible that mention the Holy Spirit, both in the Old Testament and the New and I hope you will enjoy discovering these for yourself.

Just a couple of pointers: -

- In the book of Joel Chapter 2 verses 28-29, "I will pour out my Spirit on all people".

- In the book of Acts Chapter 2 verse 4, "And everyone present was filled with the Holy Spirit".

In order to gain a deeper understanding of these "Fruits" which the Holy Spirit grows in us, we will now look at each one separately.

1. **LOVE**

    The Greek word for "love" in this context is "agape". This love is the spiritual love that God wants us to have for each other. It is the attitude of mind that, whatever the other person is like, we will treat them with respect and desire the best for them.

Agape is also the word for God's love for us all, which He demonstrated when He gave us His only Son, Jesus Christ, to be crucified for our sins (John 3 : 16).

Most people will, of course, have different ideas as to what the word "love" means to them. For many people, it means the love that parents have for their children and grandchildren. Or perhaps for their brother or sister. Family love.

There is also the warm, considerate love between friends and colleagues.

Finally, there is the "love" between two people, often resulting in marriage/living together and involving sexual passion between them.

2. **JOY**

Another word to describe joy is "delight". This again is a spiritual attitude of mind which, no matter what your circumstances are, or whatever happens to you, you will find something positive, something to rejoice in. It is having a positive attitude to life, not a negative one, having your glass "half full" rather than "half empty".

Then you will look around at other people, and your circumstances, and find something to rejoice in - to have a sense of Joy.

3. **PEACE**

    As in the case of "Love", this word Peace has several different meanings.

    At a personal level, people are "at peace" with each other when they are not angry, arguing or fighting. Countries and tribes are "at peace" with each other when they are not at war.

    From a spiritual point of view, the Bible defines peace as perfect serenity and tranquillity, having a life and state of mind in which we are kind to each other and we are "at peace" with God.

    We must seek to follow the Christian way of life, to enjoy the total love God has for us and then receive the transcending peace from Him.

## 4. PATIENCE

There have been many occasions in my life when I have needed the "patience of a saint". Then, when I have lost my patience with something or someone, I felt angry and frustrated.

This often involves waiting for something longer than we expect. Maybe a medical or hospital appointment, or a parcel or workman to turn up, or even something else to happen in our lives. The word long-suffering comes to mind.

Perhaps this has been your experience also. All I can say is that since finding my faith I have been a lot more patient with people and situations, which has greatly improved my daily life. This is a gift of the Holy Spirit.

Patience is also the word used of God's long-suffering treatment towards us and our failings. If we want to show more patience towards others, we must first increase our understanding of God's patience with us.

## 5. KINDNESS

The first two qualities of love quoted in the Bible at 1 Corinthians 13 : 4 are "love is patient, love is kind".

So not only should we be patient with other people, we should also show kindness. Whereas patience can be non-active, for example if someone lets us down we can still be patient with them without doing anything, kindness requires some sort of action. Acts of kindness can simply be talking to someone lonely, or helping with shopping, driving, jobs in the home or garden (without payment or reward), or helping someone financially. You will also think of so many more examples.

Sending His son Jesus to die for us, and saving us, was definitely an act of kindness on the part of God. So if we can know and appreciate God's kindness towards us, we are more likely to be kind to others.

6. **GOODNESS**

Most of us think of this word as "being good at something", either in a sporting context, or at work or in the home - DIY, cooking, etc. Also, we often tell our children to "be good" at school, home or in their achievements.

But as one of the spiritual fruits, it is more akin to kindness. It refers to having a good (kind) attitude towards other people, so that we can show active and practical goodness and generosity towards them.

## 7. **FAITHFULNESS**

In the New Testament of the Bible, this often refers to "having faith in the Lord". A person with "true faith" not only accepts the blessings in Christ, but also accepts the teaching and commands of Christ.

In this modern day and age, we think of faithfulness being important in our relationships or marriage and in our work situations - A person on whose faithful service we can rely; on whose loyalty we can depend upon; on whose word we can accept and trust.

To sum up, faithfulness, as part of the fruit of the Spirit, means being faithful to God's command that patience, kindness and goodness should be displayed towards others.

## 8. **GENTLENESS**

This is a much harder word to describe or understand. It is often thought to mean being weak, or lacking energy, or being complacent. You may have heard the expression, "meek and mild".

I prefer to think of this as a state of mind and heart. To have strength and empathy under self-control.

In the New Testament of the Bible, in 2 Corinthians 10 : 1, Paul writes that Jesus Christ himself acted with gentleness and kindness. This is true of the character of Jesus and one that we should all try to aspire to.

## 9. **SELF-CONTROL**

This means that we have control over ourselves, our actions and our words we use in all situations. We are the masters of ourselves and not slaves to anger, violent or abusive behaviour. To control our habits of drinking, smoking, eating, or others.

It is very easy for humans to lose our temper, to shout abuse, to lash out uncontrollably and hurt someone. This is a very hard Fruit of the Spirit to exhibit all the time, but is still possible if we display all the previous "Fruits" mentioned.

The New Testament of the Bible refers to self-control, not only as the masters of self, but as the shaping and living of our lives in the way which God desires.

**Love, and Fruits of the Spirit, in action**

When the Covid-19 virus entered the UK, and shortly after the first "lockdown" in March 2020, many families suffered financially, with loss of work and jobs, rising debts and unable to pay regular bills. People were thrown into poverty and lack of food. Local communities all over the country rallied to provide support.

Then the Alpha Centre, Holy Trinity Church in Brompton, London started up a food box supply service, with volunteers. They called this "Love Your Neighbour". With volunteers and donations flooding in, this quickly spread to most areas of the country, with lots of churches and communities joining in.

Thousands of families have been helped with food on their tables, all delivered free of charge, with love. What a fantastic example of these

Fruits of the Spirit, of love working in our communities and country.

Could this be part of our "new normal"?

I hope that you now have a better and deeper understanding of the Holy Spirit and the Fruits of the Spirit, which I can honestly say have given me a better, more satisfying, quality of life.

This better way of life, whatever your age, can be available to you too, in fact to everyone, because this is what God wants for us all.

Why not make a start right now by searching online for Alpha UK and sign up for an online course, or speak to a local Church Leader or friend. Find out, post Covid-19 times, if there are any "face to face" Alpha courses starting soon near you.

# CHAPTER 9

# THE EXISTENCE OF GOD

I hope that I have been able to convince you, in Chapter 5, that everything written about Jesus Christ, the Son of God - His life, miracles, crucifixion and resurrection from death - is the truth. But what about God?

The first thing to say is that it is not possible to prove the existence of God in the same way that I did with Jesus Christ. There are of course many historical documents, those previously referred to, that mention the one single God, but I think we must look much wider, and all around us, to find God.

First, let us think about the past. In the distant past, people from all different nations across the world, worshiped different "gods". For example, the ancient Egyptians had more than 1500 gods to worship and they were an integral part of people's lives. You have probably seen pictures of Ra, the hawk headed Sun God and the other more commonly known were Isis, Osiris and Horus.

The ancient Greeks believed that all gods came from either the earth or the sky. They included

Zeus, the "King" god of the sky and thunder, Aphrodite the god of love and beauty, Poseidon the god of the sea, Apollo the god of music and health and Hades the God of the dead.

During the period of the Roman Empire, the Romans worshipped Jupiter, Juno, Minerva, Neptune, Venus, Mars, Apollo, Diana and others.

What is most interesting, however, is that for thousands of years the Jewish nation, the Israelites, worshipped only one true God, whose name is Yahweh. As human knowledge and understanding increased, people of the world started believing in this one God - the God we worship today.

So much for the history lesson, and I apologise if history is not your thing, but let us now consider the very reasonable arguments proving the existence of God.

Firstly, we must start with creation itself. The beginning of the Universe, the planet Earth and all forms of life. I will not go into any great detail in this book about creation as there are so many other books you can read on this subject.

I will simply explain to you what I believe is sufficient proof, from my searching, of the existence of God, the creator.

The whole universe, galaxies, planets, stars, the sun and moon, display an amazing level of interdependency. In simplest terms, our earth depends on the sun and moon being exactly the right distance away, to give us heat and light and for maintaining tides and gravity.

All the stars we can see move, not randomly, but in perfect order and position, always. Is this by chance or design?

The Earth also has just the right mixture of chemicals, gases, air and water to sustain life. The human body is designed with just the right internal organs to function.

This clearly points to the fact that our Earth was designed for human life to be possible, and nothing is random. The creator, designer, can only be our Spiritual God.

Then when the DNA Genome code was discovered, the evidence for "design" (by God) became undeniable.

The requirements to sustain life, and the scientific evidence of a complex code in the make-up of that life, led to many scientists believing in God.

So, going back to the start of all this creation, everyone would agree that if something exists, then something or someone caused it to exist. The idea that the whole universe, all the forces of nature, like gravity, all forms of life, came into existence from nothing is simply ridiculous.

Even if you go along with the "cosmic" Big Bang theory, you still have to find the cause.

When you think about the design of the human body and mind, the popular belief is that God, the creator, included moral laws to live by. Humans instinctively know, from birth, what is right and what is wrong. We know what behaviour is good and what is evil. We all have a conscience.

But we are not robots! God has also given us the freedom of choice. We are all free to do what is good, or what is evil.

More evidence for the existence of God can be found in the wonders, and life forms, of nature.

We see beauty in the formation, shapes, colours and smells of so many flowers and trees. The way that the leaves of trees soak up harmful carbon dioxide and provide oxygen vital for our planet. The way trees change with all the seasons. The sheer variety, colour and fragrance and perfect formation of flowers is another example of created beauty.

Add to this the sheer brilliance of design and complexity of millions of animals, birds, sea creatures and insects, who we humans share this earth with, can only lead to an undeniable conclusion of the existence of a wonderful, powerful God.

But you must reach your own conclusion. God did not make us robots. He does not force anyone to believe in Him. God does, however, provide the abundant proof of His existence, as I have outlined, to make it easy for us to believe. All you need do is to look up and around you.

# CHAPTER 10

# HAVING A PERSONAL RELATIONSHIP WITH GOD

By the time you reach this chapter of my book, you may well be asking the same big questions of life as I had in 2007. You may well have accepted the truth about Jesus and the existence of God, and you will know what first steps to take, and the enormous benefits to a better, happier way of life.

If this is the case, then you will definitely want to have a personal relationship with God. Remember that God loves you, that He created you and He wants the best for you. We have the same access to God as a child has to his or her father.

Because God is Spirit, He makes his home in us. His presence is always with us and we can talk to Him in prayer. We come to know God through reading the Bible, allowing Him to teach and guide us through His Spirit and accepting the gift of His son Jesus, who died for our sins so that we can receive eternal life in Heaven.

If God could write you a letter, here are some of the things He would say:-

- I know everything about you (Psalm 139 : 1)

- I am familiar with all your ways (Psalm 139:3)

- It is my desire to lavish my love on you, because you are my child and I am your Father (1 John 3 : 1)

- My plan for your future has always been filled with hope (Jeremiah 29 : 11)

- If you seek me with all your heart you will find me (Deuteronomy 4 : 29)
- I am the Father who comforts you in all your troubles (2 Corinthians 1 : 3)

- When you are broken hearted I am close to you (Psalm 34 : 18)

- Jesus died so that you and I could be reconciled (2 Corinthians 5 : 18)

These words come from the heart of God, so rejoice in the truth and give Him your thanks in prayer.

As I mentioned in Chapter 6, I had discussed on the Alpha Course how we should pray, but at first I did not find this easy. A friend of mine told me that praying is simply having a conversation with God, just like any other chat with a friend. So I imagined that God, my Father, was sitting on a chair opposite, waiting for me to talk to Him, knowing He is always ready to listen.

Of course there are times when we all struggle to pray, because we feel exhausted, sleepy, sick or weak and that's okay. God, and Jesus, loves us and is patient and forgiving towards us.

In the seventeenth century, a Frenchman by the name of Francois Fenelon wrote these words about prayer:-

- Tell God all that is in your heart - it's pleasure and it's pains - as you would to a close friend.

- Tell God your troubles, so He may comfort you.

- Tell Him your joys, so He may sober them.

- Tell Him your longings, so He may purify them.

- Talk to God of your temptations or addictions, so He may shield you from them.

- Tell God of wounds of your heart, that He may heal them.

- If you thus pour out all your weaknesses, needs and troubles, there will be no lack of what to pray.

I would just like to add to these words, we should also not forget to praise and thank God for all the gifts and blessings He gives us each day, for which there are many.

My submission is that reading the Bible, and talking to God in prayer, is the best way to have a personal relationship with God.

I discovered that by doing these two things, I have received the following benefits:

- I know that God is always with me.

- I see what life is really about.

- I am set free to be who I really am.

- Prayer makes me strong to face what I need to.

- Praying gives me the opportunity to pray for the needs of others, family and friends who are grieving, or are sick, or struggling with debt, unemployment, or other troubles in their lives.

- Prayer feeds and nourishes my spiritual life.

- Prayer brings me joy and an experience of God's power, love and glory.

In concluding this chapter, an American Pastor and Author wrote, "For the miracle of prayer to begin operating in your life, we must finally do only one thing. We must pray. I can write about prayer and you can read about it, but sooner or later we have to pray. Then, and only then, will we begin to live moment by moment in God's presence."

# CHAPTER 11

# WHAT ABOUT CHURCH?

Can I be a Christian, leading a new "Christian" way of life and not go to church?

I wonder what comes to mind when you think of church and churchgoers? Perhaps you imagine a beautiful cathedral or an old church building, with Priests and Ministers wearing strange coloured outfits, following various rules and practices. There are very many of these to be seen in our towns and villages throughout the country. Then there are many smaller chapels, in towns and villages, which tend to be less formal, bordering on the "casual", mostly with a modern style of worship.

As I mentioned in Chapter 7, after completing the Alpha Course I decided to try out the local church. It may be that going to church regularly is not something that appeals to you, or may seem out of your comfort zone.

It cannot be denied that church attendances have slowly declined over the past 40-50 years, even though probably half the population still say they are "Christian" and believe in God and heaven!

Large numbers of people do feel a spiritual connection and, whilst not interested in church or religion, still believe that "somewhere up there" is God in heaven. This perhaps explains that when we, human beings, are in peril, danger, war, fear, we cry out to God for help. Yes, we all have this spiritual connection, our soul, whether we are aware of it or not.

The question, therefore, is, has the established institution of church fallen "behind the times", sticking to out-of-date practices and language, or have people, communities and the media, in general, found and developed other interests such as playing or watching sports on Sundays, shopping in supermarkets and centres, eating out, visiting garden centres, and so the list goes on.

I guess the answer lies somewhere between the two. The truth of the matter is that "church" is not a building at all! "Church" is made up of people, not stone, bricks and mortar. In the Bible Christians are referred to as "the body of Christ" and are the church. The early Christians who followed Jesus Christ and His teachings, would meet together in each other's houses, then as more and more people accepted Christ, and Christianity spread to other countries, larger places of worship were found, or built.

So the answer to the above question is Yes - you can believe in God, and Jesus Christ, and live your new way of life without attending a conventional, established church on a Sunday morning.

But I believe you would be missing out on so many benefits, so many joys and happiness, that are freely available in the different, better way of life we all want. The "new normal" you may be looking for, which includes church life,

We read in the Bible that we should indeed meet regularly with other believers and there are good reasons for this. Human beings were not created to live lonely, isolated lives, but to live together in fellowship, love and community.

If nothing else, the coronavirus pandemic has highlighted our need for each other and for close connection with family, friends and other human beings.

The first thing I experienced when I started attending my local church in Buckinghamshire was the warm and friendly welcome I received. I quickly made new friendships and still have these close friends in Bucks. Group meetings were, and still are, held in houses, where we encourage and support each other.

Many mid-week activities were and are enjoyed, including an art group, walking group, fishing trips, coffee mornings, summer BBQs and helping each other with cooking meals and DIY projects. So much fun to have!

Then when I moved with my wife to live in North Devon in 2014, I found the same love and friendship from Christian church communities. New friends were quickly made and groups include various craft mornings, mother and baby groups, men's breakfast club and children and youth groups. The church I now attend run Alpha Courses (as do several others) and a monthly Sunday afternoon "tea service" with sandwiches and cakes. At least two local churches also make space to play short mat bowls!

So it is clear that the people who make up the Church of God have, in fact, risen to the challenges of the 21st century and are meeting the needs and interests of the many.

If what I have said in this chapter is not a cure, a solution to loneliness, then I don't know what is.

2020 church doors were closed, but church remained very much open! Church groups and meetings went online - welcome to the world of

Church online / Alpha online / Church & Social Groups via zoom
(bring your own coffee !!) / Weddings and Funerals live streamed

Rosemarie Ayrton

# CHAPTER 12

## HOPE FOR THE FUTURE

The word HOPE has lots of different meanings and applications in our normal daily lives.

Hope is all about looking forward to a better future, or a good, positive outcome. For example, we hope for good weather when we go away on holiday, or on days out. We hope our football, rugby, cricket, or other sports teams will win their matches. We hope to recover quickly when we become sick. We hope to have enough money to pay our bills. We hope to pass exams and have a good job. We hope, hope, hope for so many things.

And of course the big hope at the time of writing is that the various vaccines for Covid-19 pandemic will reduce the number of infections and deaths, reduce the pressure on our NHS hospitals and enable people to return to some sort of "normal" life.

Then again, there is a different hope, what is called the Christian hope. Nearly everyone I talk to, Christian and non-Christian alike, say that when they die (and I repeat when, not if, as we will all die one day) they hope to go to heaven.

This is, in fact, an acknowledgement of a spiritual "afterlife", a place for our soul to enjoy everlasting life in the presence of God and Jesus Christ.

The Christian hope, or viewpoint, is that there is an existence "beyond the grave" by a resurrection, available to all. This is promised to us by Jesus Christ, who died and rose again, to defeat death itself.

When Jesus rose again, three days after His crucifixion, He appeared to many people over the course of 40 days, as the same recognisable man whom the disciples had known. There is a lot of documented evidence to prove this, with over 500 eye witnesses. Many of these witnesses were prepared to lose their own lives, rather than change their testimonies. They stuck to the truth of what they saw.

If you were sitting on a jury today and heard 500 witnesses testify to seeing the same thing, or person, what would your verdict be?

Jesus is the one who still lives and promises the hope of everlasting life in heaven, to all who believe in Him. So the message of Christianity is that we can indeed be ready to meet our maker, by ensuring we have faith in Jesus, and living a life in accordance with His teachings and commandments.

A few years ago a film was made called Hachi - A Dogs Tail ! The film told the story of a University Professor who took in a stray puppy named Hachi. Each day the professor went to work by train and the dog showed his loyalty by waiting at the train station for him to return. Then one day the professor died at work of a stroke. That day, Hachi waited at the train station for several hours. Then, for the next 10 years Hachi went to the train station every day, awaiting his loving master. What amazing loyalty and devotion.

In the Bible, there is a story written by Luke, about a man named Simeon who patiently waited for the coming of his Master, the Messiah. Eventually, when Mary and Joseph went to the Temple with the baby Jesus, Simeon held Him in his arms and knew his wait was over. You can read the full story of Simeon in Luke Chapter 2.

Jesus Christ has promised that one day He will return, to restore the world to what it was meant to be. No more pain or suffering.

In the meantime, He provides the hope and strength we all need, for each new day of our lives.

# CHAPTER 13

## CAN I REKINDLE MY FAITH ?

I have a very good friend who, unlike myself, was born into a Christian family. As a child, he was taken to church by his parents and was brought up, into his teens, believing in God and Jesus Christ. His faith was straightforward and uncomplicated.

When my friend reached his early twenties he fell in love, got married, left home and started a career to pay the mortgage and household bills. He no longer had time for God and his faith went cold.

We have had discussions about his loss of faith, contrasting it with my own discovery of faith late in life, at the age of 63.

My friend agrees that it is not too late to rekindle his Christian belief, but is still lacking in confidence and will-power to take that first step, to head back to the boat of salvation with Jesus.

Another person I know was what I call a "passive" believer, as a child and teenager. His family did not attend church, but had a belief in

God and "doing good" in their lives. He developed a love for music in his teens and learnt to play the guitar. He then joined a band, playing in a church every Sunday morning and enjoyed singing worship songs. His heart was turned to God.

A few years later, now married, he moved away to live in a different part of the country, where house prices and cost of living was lower, to help his financial position. Other interests took over in his life and his love for music, church and serving God disappeared.

But God still loves him and all people who have, for whatever reason, turned away.

Most of us have heard the well known story of The Prodigal Son. It goes like this:-

A man had two sons. The younger son told his father, "I want my share of your estate now, instead of waiting until you die". So his father agreed to divide his wealth between them. A few days later this younger son packed his bags and left. He went to a distant land, where he wasted all his money on wild living. Then a great famine swept over the land and he began to starve. He remembered that even his father's workmen had food, so he decided to return home and beg for a job. While he was still some distance away, his father saw him and, filled with love and compassion, the father ran to his son and embraced him. The son did not feel he was worthy of being his father's son, but the father gave him his best robe, a ring and sandals and prepared a feast to celebrate. The father said, "This son of mine was dead and is alive again. He was lost but now is found".

This is, in fact, one of many parables which Jesus told to crowds of people in those days.

But what is a parable? Some people think it is an earthly story with a heavenly meaning. A clearer definition could be a short, simple story on a familiar subject, from which a moral or spiritual lesson can be learnt.

There are, in fact, no less than 33 parables of Jesus in the bible books of Matthew, Mark and Luke. Some you will be very familiar with and some not so.

With some parables the meaning and lesson to be learnt is very clear and understandable, whilst others are more difficult.

These are the greatest stories ever told, teaching us moral and social behaviour and justice, how we should treat and love each other and how much God loves you and all people of the world.

The meaning of the parable of The Prodigal Son is very clear. It is that however long ago you left your "Father God" and whatever you have done whilst away, He has always loved and missed you, and always will, and will gladly welcome you back with open arms and celebrate with you.

So the answer to the question, "Can I rekindle my faith?" is a resounding YES. It is never too late!

All you need do is to mentally turn back, like the prodigal son (or daughter) and take the first steps on the road to home. Perhaps your first step could be looking into attending an Alpha Course, or doing Alpha online from home.

If you would like to read some or all of the parables of Jesus, but not sure where to find them in the Bible, I have included a list of these as Appendix 2 at the back of this book.

# CHAPTER 14

## IN CONCLUSION - YOUR FUTURE STARTS NOW

This last chapter is written for all those readers who still have an inquisitive mind and wish to investigate further the way to finding a new and better way of living.

Whether your life, so far, has been trouble free and "plain-sailing" or full of pain (perhaps somewhere in between) there comes a point in all our lives when you begin to feel there has to be more to life.

The Covid-19 pandemic has brought into sharp focus all the things we human beings need, want and desire. Things we dearly miss when they are taken away:-

- Spending time, and hugs, with distant family and friends

- Shopping and social trips

- Playing or supporting sports activities

- Theatre and cinema trips

- Going away on holidays

- Attending church for worship/other activities

- Going to pubs, restaurants and cafes

- AND - our loss of freedom

There are, however, many benefits that the coronavirus has given to us:-

- Having more time at home with the people we live with, partners and children

- A "quieter" life, appreciating the sounds of nature and birdsong

- Greater appreciation of the role in our society of essential workers, particularly the NHS, doctors, nurses, care homes, household waste collectors, delivery drivers and many more

- Communities coming together with help, support and love for each other

- Greater concern for the world we live in

- Huge increase in the number of people seeking spiritual comfort and guidance – in other words, seeking God

Many people have been asking, "What is the new normal going to look like?". Perhaps you could pick out from the above two lists, the things you would like to include in your new, post Covid-19, way of life. Then add a few more of your own.

We cannot rely entirely on our politicians or Government, we have to make our own future way of living.

The good news is that Jesus Christ can, and will, help us in this task. In Chapter 7 I explained how the Holy Spirit changed my life and what the Holy Spirit does. The Holy Spirit is that part of God that Jesus promises to us, to live within us and be our helper and guide. All you have to do is simply ask Jesus, ask the Holy Spirit, to prepare and disclose to you the new and better way of life you desire.

You can do this any time, any day, any place; there is really nothing stopping you from taking your first step towards your new, better life.

Simply Google Alpha UK and take a look. What have you got to lose?

Do this with an open mind, and be willing for your heart, eyes and ears to receive divine guidance, then your pathway to joy, happiness and comfort will open up.

The fact you are reading this book is a clear sign that God is seeking you out. He is calling your name, because you are "the special one" to Him.

I hope that this book will encourage you to start your own exciting journey into your future. Seek and you will find.

It is never too late !

When we are younger, in our teens and twenties, we all have dreams and aspirations. For some people these are achieved, but for many, dreams become our failures. So we make new dreams and plans and if by the time we are in our 30s to 50s and they have not come to fruition, we experience moments of greater failure - a mid-life crisis.

It is then easy to believe that it's too late for us - that we have lost our chance at a life of purpose and self-worth.

But the promises you made to yourself previously have not been totally lost. When you begin to understand the good news of God's love for you, through Jesus Christ, you will realise IT IS NOT TOO LATE, and God still has a purpose and a future for you.

# APPENDIX 1

# THE SONG

1. When I was small
   my daddy said to me,
   Work hard at school
   and go get a degree.
   Cos you're in the system -
   Yes you are, you're in the system now.

2. Then you are told
   to work from 9 to 5,
   Then work some more
   just to stay alive.
   You're in the system now,
   Don't forget, you're in the system now.

3. But God knows, God knows
   you want to break free.
   I want to say no,
   this system is bad.
   There must be more
   from the life I have had.
   God knows, God knows, I want to break free.

4. You get a house
   and a mortgage too,
   Get loads of debts,
   now the pressure's on you.

You're in the system now,
Yes you are, you're in the system now.

5. There's no time for God,
no time to pray,
Trapped in the system,
Satan's got his way.
Trapped in the system now,
Yes you are - trapped in the system now.

6. But you can break free,
Just pray every day,
Put your trust in Jesus,
He will show you the way.
Cos God knows, God knows you want to break free.

7. It's strange but it's true,
you now have the Holy Spirit in you,
You have broken away,
God is with you every day.
You have escaped the system !

Note:

Verses 1,2,4 and 5 can be sung to the tune of You're in the Army now

Verses 3,6 and 7 can be sung to the tune of I want to break free.

# APPENDIX 2

## THE PARABLES OF JESUS

The following chart lists important parables of Jesus Christ

| PARABLE | MATTHEW | MARK | LUKE |
|---|---|---|---|
| The Lamp | 5:14-16 | 4:21-25 | 8:16-18 |
| The Speck and The Log | 7:1-5 | | 6:37-42 |
| New Cloth on Old Garment | 9:16-17 | 2:21-22 | 5:36-39 |
| The Divided Kingdom | 12:24-30 | 3:23-27 | 11:14-23 |
| The Sower | 13:1-23 | 4:1-20 | 8:4-15 |
| The Growing Seed | | 4:26-29 | |
| The Good Samaritan | | | 10:29-37 |
| The friend at Midnight | | | 11:5-13 |
| The Rich Fool | | | 12:13-21 |
| The Barren Fig Tree | | | 13:6-9 |
| The Weeds Among the Wheat | 13:24-30 | | |
| The Mustard Seed | 13:31-332 | 4:30-34 | 13:18-19 |
| The Leaven | 13:33-34 | | 13:20-21 |
| Hidden Treasure | 13:44 | | |
| Pearl of Great Price | 13:45-46 | | |
| The Net | 13:47-50 | | |
| The Invited Guests | | | 14:7-14 |
| The Heart of Man | 15:10-20 | 7:14-23 | |
| The Lost Sheep | 18:10-14 | | 15:1-7 |
| The Lost Coin | | | 15:8-10 |
| The Prodigal Son | | | 15:11-32 |
| The Rich Man and Lazarus | | | 16:19-31 |
| The Persistent Widow | | | 18:1-8 |
| The Pharisee and The Publican | | | 18:9-14 |
| The Unforgiving Servant | 18:23-35 | | |
| Labourers in the Vineyard | 20:1-16 | | |
| The Two Sons | 21:28-32 | | |
| The Tenant Farmers | 21:33-45 | 12:1-12 | 20:9-19 |
| Marriage Feast or Great Banquet | 22:1-14 | | 14:15-24 |
| The Budding Fig Tree | 22:32-35 | 13:28-33 | 21:29-33 |
| The Faithful vs. The Wicked Servant | 24:45-51 | 13:34-37 | 12:35-48 |
| The Ten Virgins | 25:1-13 | | |
| Ten Talents or Gold Coins | 25:14-30 | | 19:11-27 |

# APPENDIX 3

For further information – some online resources:

www.alphacourse.org

www.christianity.org.uk

www.christianityexplored.org

www.premier.org.uk


Last, but by no means least, if when reading this book you still feel confused or worried and have any questions, you can contact the author by email to smithstanley390@gmail.com.

Printed in Great Britain
by Amazon